IMAGES
of America

SOUTHWICK
REVISITED

[Southwick]

A Plan of the Town of Southwick, 1795. This is the earliest known map of Southwick, which is oriented with north to the right. In the upper right (northwest) is Munn Brook, which bends at roughly a right angle, while Great Brook is the dark line going from the southwest end of Middle Pond north into Westfield. The dotted line at top is present-day Loomis Street. The one in the middle is College Highway. Branching off it to the east is Feeding Hills Road. The dotted line west from College Highway is part of Klaus Anderson Road, Curtis Road, a closed section of road, and the old Sodom Mountain Road. Only the Middle and North Ponds of the Congamond Lakes are shown. The present-day southern "jog" of Southwick was part of Connecticut from 1774 to 1804, which explains the straight Connecticut line and why South Pond is not included in this plan. (Massachusetts State Archives.)

On the Cover: Frank Noble, 1872. Seated in his carriage, Frank Noble is joined by other family members. He eventually distributed prepackaged popcorn and became known as the "Popcorn Man." (Southwick Historical Society.)

IMAGES
of America

SOUTHWICK
REVISITED

Lee David Hamberg for the
Celebrate Southwick 250 Committee

ARCADIA
PUBLISHING

Published by Arcadia Publishing
Charleston, South Carolina

Printed in the United States of America

Library of Congress Control Number: 2020946943

For all general information, please contact Arcadia Publishing:
Telephone 843-853-2070
Fax 843-853-0044
E-mail sales@arcadiapublishing.com
For customer service and orders:
Toll-Free 1-888-313-2665

Visit us on the Internet at www.arcadiapublishing.com

*Dedicated to Patricia L. Odiorne and the late Gilbert S. Arnold,
two local historians who have preserved much of our town's heritage.*

CONTENTS

ACKNOWLEDGMENTS

The Celebrate Southwick 250 Committee believed in this project and allocated funds to see that it happened. The Historical Content Work Group of the committee, consisting of Samuel and Charlene Goodwin, Todd Shiveley, David Pierce, Gae Strong Freniere, Juliette Mason, and Sue Zidek, have been extremely supportive.

Since 1971, when the Southwick Historical Society was organized, its primary goal has been to collect local history. Household items and farm tools have been preserved in the Southwick History Museum at 86 College Highway. There are also hundreds of photographs, newspapers, and documents. Many of these latter items have been acquired since *Around Southwick* was released by Arcadia Publishing in 1997. To the people who have donated them, a sincere thank-you. The majority of the images in this book are a direct result of those gifts.

Many individuals in the past year have shared photographs and other items. David Gunn provided Fowler family items. Patricia L. Odiorne, former archivist for the society, located other images. Juliette Mason had photographs of the VFW and its auxiliary the North Pond, and the 1955 flood. Carole Olson shared family photographs from around the Congamond Lakes, while Jim Putnam had pictures of his family's farm. Mark Rankin shared from his Southwick ephemera, and Todd Shively had taken some great photographs. The files of the historical commission were used, while David Pierce took photographs in the Old Cemetery and of several homes. Barbara and Marcus Phelps shared from their archives, while Sandra (Miller) Jablonski had some family photographs. The Springfield *Republican* thinned out its archives, and historian Joseph Carvalho III made them available to museums in the area. Buzz Caron of Southwoods Printing also contributed time and images.

Numerous other individuals assisted. Martin Lee and Cole Ludorf did scanning. Gene Theroux provided veteran information and digital editing. Carol Geryk, Patricia Odiorne, Jim Putnam, and Sue Zidek reviewed every caption for accuracy and readability. The Southwick Civic Fund provided administrative and financial support. The staff at Arcadia has been a pleasure to work with. I want to give thanks to my wife, Dodie, and my children, who encouraged and, at times, tolerated my historical passions over many years. Thank you!

Images are courtesy of the Southwick Historical Society, unless indicated as follows: Richard Battistoni (RB); Marie Boccasile (MB); Phyllis Gonska Bombard (PGB); Nelson Buzz Caron (NBC); Christ Church, United Methodist (CCUM); Matthew Egerton (ME); David Gunn (DG); Lee David Hamberg (LDH); Sandra Jablonski (SJ); Carol and Clyde Jones (C&CJ); Juliette Mason (JM); Massachusetts State Archives (MSA); Carole Olson (CO); David Pierce (DP); Pioneer Valley Live Steamers (PVLS); Marcus and Barbara Phelps (M&BP); Don and Nancy Prifti (D&NP); Jim Putnam (JP); Mark Rankin (MR); Todd Shively (TS); Southwick town clerk's office (STC); Springfield Armory, NPS (SA, NPS); and Springfield *Republican* (SR).

Thank you to all who loaned materials for this publication.

INTRODUCTION

In 1955, Maud Gillett Davis wrote *Historical Facts and Stories About Southwick*, which is still the only major town history. The Southwick Historical Society sells copies of that manuscript, as well as an every-name index compiled by Patricia Odiorne. In 1970, at the 200th anniversary of Southwick, *Bicentennial Book* was published, which relied heavily on the work of Davis but included several chapters that went beyond her work. *Around Southwick* (1997) was a watershed because it included many previously unpublished pre–World War II photographs.

This volume is based almost exclusively on images that were previously unpublished. There are people, places, and events depicted here that are virtually unknown. Other images are recognizable as local landmarks. There are some very old photographs and a few new images to fill a void. It is hoped that history will prove the value of all of these images.

Everything could not be included. Some photographs were either not available or not forthcoming. History often has holes because the typical scenes of life go unrecorded, are tossed out, or, today, are gone forever with a simple push of the "delete" key.

What is in this volume? Many early- and mid-20th-century snapshots, taken by locals, who never intended them to be published. Sometimes the quality was extraordinary, sometimes less so. They all depict everyday life in Southwick. There are houses and barns, hay and tobacco, horses, and tractors and trucks. All of this reflects the agrarian life that was vital to this town. There are parade floats, both horse-drawn and vehicle-pulled, numerous town organizations, and headstones of long-gone citizens, as well as folks still seen in town. There are also depictions of the 1955 flood, which did more damage in Southwick than any other natural disaster. Not to include these more recent photographs would be to leave large holes in the historical fabric of this town.

Many photographs in previous publications had captions with the names of every person shown. A majority of those were taken by professional photographers, whose group photographs were likely to be labeled. Local residents also made an effort to identify people. In this publication, a higher percentage were taken by amateur photographers for their own or their family's use. They knew the names of every individual pictured without a caption or name scribbled on the back. Today that is not the case, and many a person in these pages is, sadly, anonymous. They have been included just the same because a sense of time and place is still preserved in their picture.

The process of putting together this reflection of community life required combing through the archives of the historical society and soliciting photographs from area residents. In total, thousands of photographs, documents, and pictures were examined. Roughly 680 images were digitized, and out of that, a little over 200 were chosen. The winnowing process was difficult. It was also painful to hear of more photographs, negatives, slides, and media that were available, but not in time for publication. In conclusion, it is hoped that you, the reader, enjoy this slice of Americana. If you have corrections or happen to know something about the people, places, or events pictured, contact the Southwick Historical Society, which will be archiving either the originals or electronic copies.

One

THE HEART OF THE TOWN

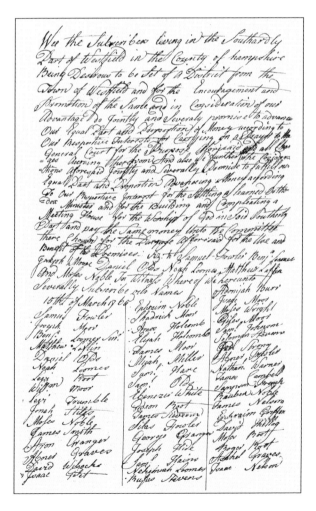

PETITION OF SEPARATION, 1765.
At the heart of a democracy is the right to petition. Southwick was initially the southern part of Westfield. In 1758, citizens in the "south part" petitioned the Westfield Town Meeting to be a district, and in 1761, a boundary was debated, with no resolution. On March 18, 1765, a second petition, seen here, was presented at a town meeting. An out-of-town boundary committee was appointed in 1767, a 1769 committee report was accepted, and the colonial legislature established the district of Southwick on November 7, 1770. (STC.)

SOUTHWICK HOTEL, C. 1900. Every town had a tavern. This one at 479 College Highway, according to Maud Davis, was constructed about 1780 by Saul Fowler. He was the son of a Westfield tavern owner. The right wing is the older section, while the left side was built in the late-first or early-second quarter of the 1800s. The integrity of the porch was good, considering the horse and rider posing on it. The barn to its immediate right may have been used to stable horses overnight. The buildings burned in 1905.

HOTEL SOUTHWICK, C. 1920. The present building at 479 College Highway was constructed in 1906 for Harry Lamb. It cost $6,000, had oak woodwork and steam heat and was considered one of the best inns in the county. For decades, it has been known as the Southwick Inn. Recently, it had a major addition to the rear, new roof, replacement wrap-around porch, kitchen, access for the disabled, and major interior renovations. It is still one of the visual focal points in Southwick's center. (M&BP.)

C.A. REED GENERAL STORE, C. 1910. Built about 1800, the property at 478 College Highway still retains its residential character. To the left is a carriage shed, the side porch is open, and the addition to the far right is lacking. By this time, the post office and the first telephone switchboard were found here. Seymour Granger converted it to a combination store and residence. The dirt roads predate College Highway, which was built about 1922–1923 and dedicated on May 22, 1923. The building is presently known as Country Colonial, specializing in early American style furniture and home decor. (LDH.)

ROLL OF HONOR, c. 1920. In 1918–1919, a temporary wooden sign was erected on the town common to recognize Southwick World War I veterans. In the left background is the Dickinson Grammar School, about where the New Fellowship Hall of the Congregational Church is. This sign was retired by 1935 when the center portion of the granite war memorial was installed. (LDH.)

SOUTHWICK HONOR ROLL, c. 1945. Located on the town common, it was constructed in 1942, only a few months after the Japanese attack on Pearl Harbor. The town expended $180 for the honor roll and an additional $6 for its repair in the following year. This is one of two known photographs of this monument. (M&BP.)

STREET VIEW, SOUTHWICK, C. 1925. Looking north toward the center, the most impressive feature was the mature elm trees, which formed a continuous canopy over the newly paved College Highway. Dutch elm disease, which was introduced into Ohio in imported logs in 1930, eventually killed virtually every American elm tree in the country. Only a handful of mature elms survive today in Southwick. (SHS.)

GAS STATION, 481 COLLEGE HIGHWAY, 1940s. Said to have been built in the 1910s, this was one of the earliest gas stations in Southwick. The man could be Clarence Hawley, who ran the station for years. With the paving of College Highway in 1923, gas stations popped up all along the route, creating a "gasoline alley." Most quickly went out of business. This one survived because of its central location. In the 1940s, it was demolished and replaced by one a few feet farther north. For years, that one was run by Walt Fiala, who, with his wife, Lynn, also ran the Southwick Inn.

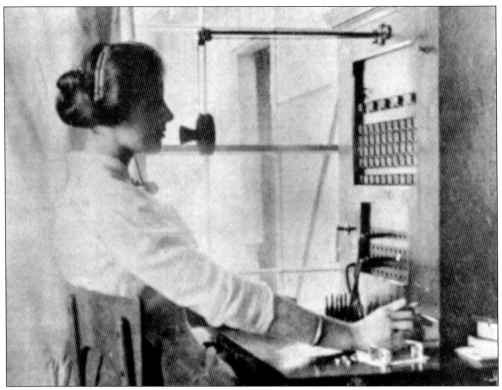

OPERATOR JANE TUTTLE, C. 1914. While telephones in Western Massachusetts date to 1877, the first telephone service in Southwick was in Charles A. Reed's store, around 1905. When Etta Reed could not handle the volume, the agency was moved to Jasper Vining's home at 435 College Highway, sometime prior to 1914. In that year, a tenant living with the Vinings, Jane (Sathory) Tuttle, became the operator. There were 45 lines in town. For years, she was known as "the telephone company" in Southwick. (LDH.)

Special

TELEPHONE DIRECTORY

for

SOUTHWICK, MASS.
(JO rdan 9)

AFTER 7:00 A. M.

WEDNESDAY, JUNE 9, 1954

Use This Directory for Southwick (JO rdan 9) Calls

PLEASE KEEP THE CURRENT
WESTFIELD DIRECTORY FOR
CALLS TO OTHER EXCHANGES

TELEPHONE DIRECTORY COVER FOR SOUTHWICK, 1954. On June 9, 1954, Southwick started dial phone service. The first call was placed by Southwick selectman Harold H. Hamberg to Cooley A. Griffin, the town's oldest telephone subscriber. There were 450 lines serving 978 stations, meaning that many families were on party lines. The present telephone building, without operators, is just north of Mrs. Murphy's Donuts at 542 College Highway.

Edward Gillett with Rhododendrons.
Starting in the late 1870s, Edward Gillett
began growing wild ferns and flowers, which
blossomed into a mail-order business with
demand from across the country and around
the world. His annual catalogs were published
for individuals, botanical gardens, and
nurserymen who wanted to cultivate native
plants. This view shows an older Edward
Gillett under a pergola or frame with birch
branches and possibly netting.

**Stock Certificate, Gillett Fern and
Flower Farm, 1944.** In 1926, Edward
Gillett turned over the business to his son
Kenneth, who died suddenly in 1932. It then
went to grandson Kenneth Jr. When he
died at age 27 in 1942, the business went to
the grandson's brother Thornton Richard
Gillett and mother, Violet S. Gillett. On
July 11, 1944, 2nd Lt. Thornton Richard
Gillett, co-pilot of a B-24 Liberator bomber,
was killed over France. This stock certificate
represents one of the last transactions prior to
Thornton's death. The farm was sold in 1948.

First Baptist Church of Southwick, c. 1910. There were Baptists in Southwick prior to the American Revolution, but not until 1805 did they separate from the Suffield, Connecticut, church. In 1821–1822, they constructed a meetinghouse in the vicinity of 505 College Highway. The church was active for years, but in the early 1900s the membership declined. It disbanded, and the building was purchased on May 5, 1930, by Helen (Osborne) Storrow of Boston. She had it dismantled and gifted it to the Eastern States Exposition in West Springfield, where it is now used as part of the Storrowton Tavern.

STEEPLEJACK AT WORK, CONGREGATIONAL CHURCH, 1997. This view of the Congregational church steeple shows the precarious profession of the steeplejack. Repairing, gilding, roofing, flashing, and painting of steeples, spires, and other elevated parts of buildings are the domain of this specialized trade. Dave P. Hamblin of Brimfield is the steeplejack pictured here. When this building was constructed in 1824, there undoubtedly were several carpenters and painters who used a simpler method, a ship's bosun's chair, to complete their task. (SR.)

REPLACING THE COLUMNS ON THE CONGREGATIONAL CHURCH, LATE MAY 1950. After 125 years, the columns, platform, and steps of the Congregational church were replaced. This view shows the new cast stone steps, platform, and one column in place. "Granville, Mass." is written on the front of the trailer. Days earlier, on Tuesday, May 16, a bundle with two letters that had been left by the original workmen in November 1824 fell out of the old north column. It listed the cost of the building ($6,000) and the names of the contractors and workmen.

INTERIOR OF CONGREGATIONAL CHURCH, C. 1892. In 1891, Rev. David L. Kebbe became the 19th minister. Early in his ministry, the members voted to remove the old box pews, pulpit, and pulpit chairs and replace them with curved oak pews and a modern pulpit with chairs to match. New kerosene lamps were also purchased. This view shows the completed renovations. While many considered the removal of the original furnishings sacrilegious, the majority felt that the changes represented an improvement.

BATTISTONI LUMBER & HARDWARE CO., EARLY 1950s. The Battistoni name has been associated with lumber in Southwick since the 1920s. In 1947 or 1948, this brick and block building at 503 College Highway was constructed as its hardware store. Today, the Battistoni family continues in the lumber and hardware business, with Richard Battistoni operating Interstate Building Supply. The Driving Image—a speed, off-road, and custom automotive store—is currently in this location. (RB.)

RAILROAD BRIDGE, GREAT BROOK. When the Hampshire & Hampden Railroad was initially built through Southwick, part of the track south of Depot Street, including the crossing of Great Brook, was elevated on a series of wooden trestles to avoid flooding. In the late 1880s, the trestles were removed and replaced with fill, and Great Brook was crossed on a new arched stone bridge. Note the keystone at the top of the arch. (TS.)

OUTHOUSE BEHIND JOSEPH ROCKWELL HOUSE, 1983. Beginning in the early 20th century, indoor plumbing, including bathrooms with toilets, became the American standard. This small privy, perhaps large enough to be a "two-holer," survives behind the Rockwell House at 17 Depot Street, but in a decaying state. It probably dates to 1890–1915. With a window for illumination and a lower rear wall, which was undoubtedly hinged to allow for ease of cleaning the pit or removable bin, it was intended to make the task as easy and sanitary as possible. Exclusive of farm outhouses, this is the last surviving one in town.

PAINTING OF THE FLETCHER GRISTMILL. This winter scene of the mill depicts millwright William Fletcher, a wagon loaded with bags of flour, and a team of horses covered with blankets. Two or more cart roads to the mill are indicated, and in the background is the old arched stone bridge over Great Brook, which partially collapsed in 2008 and was replaced the following year.

The Home of
Old Mill Brands

OLD MILL BRANDS LOGO. From the opposite perspective, this view of the same mill was used on the company letterhead and flour sacks in the early 1900s. The feeder canal in the foreground culminates in a grate to keep branches from entering the mill. There was a 22-foot drop to the vertical wheel that powered the grindstones. This was the last old-fashioned mill operating in Massachusetts at the time. When the dam upstream was breached in 1936, it was not repaired, and operations ceased. The mill was destroyed by fire in July 1955.

SOUTHWICK DEPOT, NORTH OF DEPOT STREET, WEST OF POWDER MILL ROAD. Located on the west side of the tracks, this edifice replaced an earlier red one-room wood-frame station. The early-1900s photograph postcard is one of very few images of the depot. The station was constructed sometime between 1887 and 1890, when Fanny Gilbert was agent. Eugene Hoffman was appointed station agent in 1890 and lived in the second-floor rooms of the new station. Passenger service was discontinued about 1932, and the depot was demolished shortly before World War II. (LDH.)

Two

BUSINESSES

BERKSHIRE ICE COMPANY STORE. Constructed in 1906 at a cost of $2,500, this edifice was a company store. The horse-drawn wagon and buggy suggest this view dates to the late 1900s or 1910s. Locals who have owned or run this store include members of the Malone, Balch, Bonini, Cahill, Grimaldi, Secora, and Shea families. The oldest section is presently a coffee shop/deli/ restaurant known as Red Riding Hood's Basket. Several sections to the west, as well as a separate building, have been added. (M&BP.)

CLYDE JONES, C. 1940. From the parking lot of Ocean State Job Lot, this view is looking north from where CVS pharmacy is now. To the far left is the C.J. Gillett cigar factory, relocated to the Southwick History Museum. The double barn was dismantled and rebuilt in Granville. Clyde Jones lived beyond the Methodist church, at top right. His father, Charles, owned the A&P, or Southwick Grocery Store, at 491 College Highway. Clyde worked there, served in Korea, and in the 1960s partnered in the building of the Village Green Shopping Plaza, where he and his wife, Carol, ran the new Jones's Supermarket. (C&CJ.)

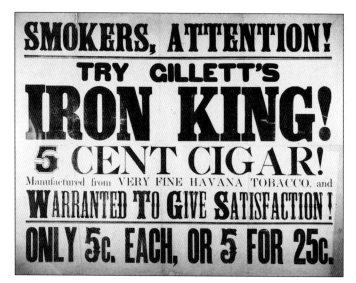

GILLETT'S IRON KING CIGAR POSTER. Charles J. Gillett was the largest cigar maker in town, initially operating his business out of the second floor of his 7 Vining Hill Road home. In 1872, he built a four-story cigar factory. Huge quantities of cigars were made there over the course of decades. In addition to Iron King, he also sold cigars under the names Eastern Train, Old States Prison, Queen Anne, Sporting Friends, and Gillett's Standard.

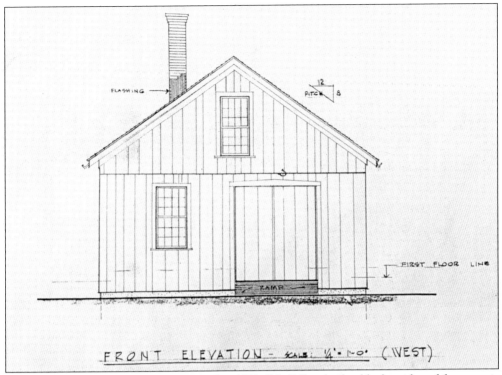

FRONT ELEVATION - SCALE ¼" = 1'-0" (WEST)

GILLETT BLACKSMITH SHOP. Sometime after 1872, C.J. Gillett built a blacksmith and farm repair shop to the southeast. The late George Steere remembered Gillett's son-in-law Frank Skinner doing farm-related repairs there. The front elevation above shows the building as it looked when first completed. The cross-section and elevation of the forge below give a better idea of the setup inside. The drawings were made shortly before the building was razed.

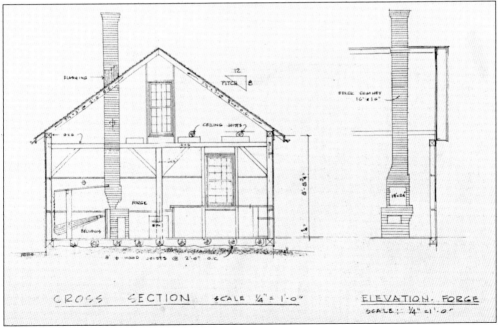

CROSS SECTION SCALE ¼" = 1'-0"

ELEVATION. FORGE
SCALE: ¼" = 1'-0"

GILLETT'S SERVICE STATION, 1939. Arthur Gillett purchased the southeast corner of College Highway and Congamond Road and had a service station built there in 1939. In this image, the building is nearing completion, although it has not been graded yet. There is still a plank for walking into the store, and the gas pumps have not been installed. Berkeley Van Mater and his son Bob owned the station from 1954 to 1977. It has been replaced by two generations of self-service Pride gas stations and a convenience store in 2014.

ARTHUR GILLETT, c. 1950. Gillett stands in front of his service station, looking like the working man that he was. The gas pumps are replacements from what was originally installed. Within a few years, the station was sold to the Van Mater family.

VALLEY INN, C. 1921. At 2 Klaus Anderson Road was the Valley Inn, built in the early 1900s and owned and operated by Fannie and Frank Lambson. In addition to providing rooms, it also sold some convenience store items. From 1936 to 1947, it was owned by Albert "Al" Reinert (1904–1982), the town blacksmith, who tore down several barns and built the present shed-roof outbuilding for his shop. After his ownership, the inn was used as a dormitory for female tobacco workers during the summers, which explains its present steel fire escape. (KS.)

VALLEY INN GARAGE, C. 1920. Opposite the Valley Inn on Klaus Anderson Road was the Valley Inn Garage in a converted barn. It sold Diamond Tires, a popular brand. The automobile is driving south on what is now College Highway. The white building with three windows is the former Root District Schoolhouse at 21 Klaus Anderson Road. The garage, which no longer exists, was immediately behind or replaced by the Valley Inn filling station at 365 College Highway, now Re-Inspired. (KS.)

GAS STATION, 726 COLLEGE HIGHWAY, MARCH 1982. Razed in 1986, this gas station at 726 College Highway was one of the last in Southwick from the 1920s and 1930s that retained period pumps. The pump on the left was a Tokheim Model 850 with a clock-face dial, or Volumeter, from 1930–1939. Bert M. Parker owned the property at the time and ran the station. To the rear of the filling station was a barn with a cupola and the Luther Fowler homestead. Presently, there is a single-story ranch home here.

Noble's Popcorn Box, 1908. Frank W. Noble was a successful Southwick entrepreneur. He started out selling his own produce, then that of his neighbors, and then tobacco, eventually building a warehouse. He then specialized in popcorn, purchasing large quantities in the West, which were shelled, cleaned, and sent in bulk. At his own warehouse, he packaged one-half and one-pound boxes of popcorn for the grocery trade. Almost a hundred years before Orville Redenbacher, Noble was known as the "Popcorn Man."

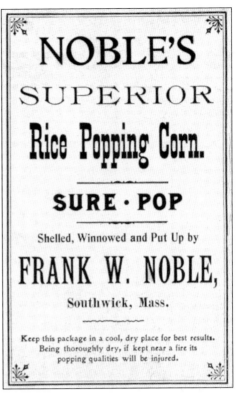

Pioneer Dairy Company Milk Bottle. Charles Nutter started the Pioneer Dairy Company in 1920 in a building only 22 by 24 feet, delivering 14 quarts of milk his first day. Over the years, it grew into an iconic Southwick business, processing and selling thousands of gallons of milk daily, as well as other dairy products and its popular fudgesicles. Numerous area stores and schools sold its products. This bottle has "Pioneer Dairy Co. Southwick, Mass." on one side and a Dutch maid on the other side. The plant closed in 2004. (LDH.)

SKI JUMP, LAMBSON'S HILL, C. 1930S. For generations, the southwest corner of Loomis Street and Granville Road was owned by the Lambson family. From the early 1900s to around 1980, shade tobacco was the primary crop on the farm. Lorenzo "L.D." Lambson not only grew tobacco, but also built the nine-hole Hilltop Golf Course, as well as a ski area with a ski jump at the foot of Sodom Mountain. According to the late Jim Montovani, the ski jump was destroyed by a storm before it could be used.

L. SUZIO TRAP ROCK CO. QUARRY, C. 1978. In the fall of 1931, the L. Suzio Trap Rock Company started building a plant on Provin Mountain. By spring it was in operation, blasting and crushing tons of trap rock for road material. A single blast in 1938 lifted 250,000–300,000 tons of stone. The shock wave was felt for miles. Henry Altobello was the president and plant manager. The quarry ceased operations by 1954, when it was bought by the John S. Lane and Son Corporation. The photograph shows the huge crusher house. It burned a few years later. (LDH.)

STATE LINE FILLING STATION, C. 1936. This postcard view shows the combination gas station, convenience store, and restaurant within a few years of the business opening in 1934. The sign to the right advertises the price of gas at 16¢ a gallon. The business added beer and wine later, and after 86 years, it is still operating today as the State Line Bar and Grill.

SOUTHWICK GOLF CLUB, C. 1950. The Southwick Country Club was the first golf course in town. The restaurant and bar were in the former Luther Fowler House, built in 1914, and the 18-hole course spanned both sides of College Highway. This postcard shows the clubhouse to the rear left of the Fowler House. At least part of the course is said to have opened in 1926. The property was sold for development in February 2018. Construction started later that year, and the buildings were razed at the end of 2019. (LDH.)

BROOKSIDE SANDWICH SHOP, C. 1925. Located where Crepes Tea House is now at 157 Feeding Hills Road, the Brookside was aptly named. This postcard shows the original building, two gas pumps, and a Gulf sign. Before a section of Great Brook was relocated toward the east, it ran so close to the rear of the building that one could "spit into it." The original building was razed and replaced in the 1950s. Numerous restaurants and bars have been in this building over the years, including Club 57, the Stumble Inn, Tumble Inn, Brookside, Brew Two, and D'Georgio's.

INTERSTATE BUILDING SUPPLY, 1976. Taken just prior to its completion, this photograph shows the business at 631 College Highway with the protruding steelwork and no roof at the main entrance. Richard Battistoni had the foresight to construct this new generation of home center. (RB.)

Three

HOMES

SAMUEL FOWLER HOUSE, C. 1940. With a 1734 plaque, the Samuel Fowler House at the southwest corner of College Highway and Sunnyside Road was said to have been the oldest house in Southwick. The original rear ell, which was torn down in the 1930s, probably dated to that period. The rear of the main section dated to the 1750s or early 1760s, and the front of the main section dated to the early 1800s. On Saturday, February 19, 1977, the house was gutted by fire and was subsequently razed. (DG.)

Capt. David Fowler House, March 1973. The Capt. David Fowler House was one of the most iconic colonial homes in Southwick, with its saltbox roof, 12-over-12 window sashes, and overhangs on the gable ends. It had a date plaque of 1747. Beginning in 1933, Lilliam Guyton called it "Ye English House" and ran a dining room with home-cooked meals. It was dismantled in the 1970s. The Wynnfield Circle adult condominium community was constructed on this site.

Richard Dickinson House, 1975. At the northwest corner of College Highway and Coes Hill Road, this home was probably built during the late 1700s. The earliest known owner of the house was Richard Dickinson, who left about $17,000 to the Town of Southwick for the support of education. Timbers and other elements were salvaged when the house was razed to allow for the construction of Interstate Building Supply. This view shows its well-braced timber frame. (RB.)

JOSEPH FORWARD HOUSE, C. 1930. Joseph Forward moved from East Granby, Connecticut, to Southwick in about 1786, which is the time of construction for this home and tavern at 301 College Highway, owned by the Deveno family. It had a ballroom across the second-floor rear and a barroom in the front center room of the second floor, as indicated by wrought iron ceiling hooks. The woman in white to the right of the huge elm tree was Ellen (Anderson) Johnson, and the photographer was her sister Elsie (Anderson) Hamberg. (LDH.)

NOBLE FOWLER HOUSE, C. 1913. Built in 1790, the Noble Fowler House at approximately 739 College Highway was one of at least four 18th-century Fowler family homes built in the north-central, or Poverty Plains, section of Southwick. In 1914, Luther Fowler built a new house next to this one, and upon its completion, the old homestead was torn down. The farm was later developed into the Southwick Country Club. The family lost the property during the Depression, and the new residence was used for golf-related functions. (DG.)

NILS LARSON HOUSE, C. 1906. At 72 Mort Vining Road, this was a common house type when constructed about 1800. The main section consisted of a couple of rooms on the first floor, with a low attic that allowed for some storage or a loft for youths to sleep in. A single-story rear ell provided additional space. The front of this house was razed about 1910, and a two-story colonial revival was built for $800 and attached to the surviving ell. Larson's numerous daughters lived in a former milk house to the rear during the demolition/construction project. (LDH.)

SMITH HOUSE, C. 1926. Located at 388 College Highway across from Bugbee Road, the 1854 Hampden County map lists L. Smith as the owner. The simple design, eaves two feet above the first floor, and a low-pitched roof suggest it was built about 1800. George Millot Jr.'s wife, Ellen (Washburn) Millot, is pictured with their five children Bertha, Dorothy, Stanley, Marjorie, and Shirley. The herdsman for the adjacent Glad-Ayr Dairy Farm lived here with his family in the late 1950s and early 1960s. The house was razed in the mid-1960s.

RISING-SARAT HOUSE, 1976. Built around 1800, the Rising-Sarat House, at the top of Coes Hill Road on the north side, was an early Cape Cod–style home. This example had a center hallway running from the front doorway to the rear room. For generations, it was owned by members of the Rising family. For most of the 1900s, it was owned by the Sarat family. It was dismantled by the Granville, Massachusetts, restoration contractor Ernie Sattler in 1986, prior to a subdivision development, but the fate of the building is uncertain.

THE BUTTON-BOX, C. 1940. Another residence built about 1800, the so-called Button-Box got its name from an antique business that was in it during the second quarter of the 20th century. It was said to have been the second house at this site. In 1991, the house was moved to 73 Vining Hill Road, and a CVS pharmacy was built on the original site in 2009–2010. The double barn and cigar factory can be seen in the background.

AMASA HOLCOMB HOUSE, C. 1890–1900. Until its fiery demise in the winter of 1918 or 1919, this was the most historic house in town. From 1828 to about 1840, Amasa Holcomb manufactured the first telescopes in the United States in this double house. About 1840, he relocated his business to Westfield. In addition to telescopes, he made tripods and mounts, surveying instruments, and experimented with photography. In the late 1840s, he purchased 249 College Highway, at which point he stopped commercially making telescopes. The people are unidentified.

HEMAN LAFLIN HOUSE, 1877. Marcus Phelps, owner of 20 Depot Street, died in November 1876. This photograph was taken the following spring or summer when his widow, Susan (Smith) Phelps, was still in mourning. She is undoubtedly the woman in black, while the women to the right would have been two of her daughters. The home was built no earlier than 1808 nor later than July 1821. This is the only photograph showing the homestead with its original front portico. In a few years, it was replaced by a Victorian porch across the entire front.

ALMON GILLETT HOUSE, 1976. Built about 1820, this was a showplace with an ell and barn to the east, ornate picket fence, flower garden, maple trees, and architectural details. It left the Gillett family in 1965, and George Zedlitz built the left addition for a dairy bar with a restaurant in the old front rooms. Beginning in 1970, antique and used furniture shops known as Houston's (owned by Thomas Houston Stoudemire) and Trash or Treasures operated here. The ell and dairy bar sections were later razed, and the main house relocated back. It was razed about 2011 for a Dunkin' Donuts.

TULLER HOUSE, C. 1930. Formerly at 51 North Longyard Road, this Cape Cod–style house appears to date from about 1820–1850 because of its proportions and wide corner boards. Joel Humeston lived on this property in the early 1800s, while Gideon Stiles Jr. owned the home in 1870. The Tuller family were owners from 1900 to 1950. The original house on this site was either extensively renovated or replaced by the one pictured here. It was razed about 1976.

FRANK W. NOBLE HOUSE, C. 1872. The earliest-known photograph of a Southwick residence is that of Frank W. Noble, the "Popcorn Man," at 240 South Longyard Road. Built around 1851 for Frederick Lovatus Noble, it was one of several Noble family homes on the street. Frank W. Noble is in the carriage, while seated on the porch is his uncle William Noble. Standing in the yard from left to right are his mother, Julia Ann Noble, and cousins Ira and Horace.

STEERE HOUSE, AUTUMN 1985. Built shortly after May 1852 by Marcus Steere, the front section stood about 300 feet west of the present site. In 1876, the original homestead at 18 Vining Hill Road was in bad repair, so Steere had it taken down, and his newer house was moved by horse, rollers, rope, and capstan onto the old foundation because of better barns and wells. The kitchen and woodshed were then added to the rear and a porch to the right side. This photograph shows the home after the front door was covered over but before the present fireplace was built and the Victorian porch was removed.

FRANK LAMBSON HOUSE, C. 1915. When this photograph was taken, Frank Lambson and his wife, Fannie, had lived at 356 College Highway for some time and made several changes, including installing metal roofing, an addition to the left, a front porch, and a bay window. In just a few years, the old dusty dirt road that crossed in front of their home was replaced by the paved College Highway, and they had moved into the Valley Inn at 2 Klaus Anderson Road. (KS.)

MILLER HOME, 89 MORT VINING ROAD, C. 1960. Marjorie "Marge" (Miller) Strickland drew this charcoal sketch of her childhood home. Marge, Sandra, and Stu were the children of Stuart and Bertha Miller, who purchased the property in 1943. The main house was initially of one story, but the roof was jacked up and studs installed, making it two stories high. Six additions changed the character of this early-1800s home. When the Millers built a ranch home up the hill around 1963, the front portion of this house was torn off, and the remainder was used as a shed. In about 2015, the remaining sections were razed. (LDH.)

ANDERSON HOUSE, C. 1905. 81 Vining Hill Road is one of three houses in Southwick that were moved during the 1800s. The old section with its Greek Revival triangular pediment in the gable dates from 1830–1850. This was the front of the house when it was at 195 Mort Vining Road. It was moved through the woods for Edward Steere about 1870. The kitchen ell was added after its relocation. From 1904 to 1989, three generations of Andersons owned the house and 75-acre farm. The C. August Anderson family is undoubtedly in the buggy.

NEWTON HOLCOMB HOUSE, 2019. The site at 38 Mort Vining Road was the birthplace of Amasa Holcomb (1786–1875), the telescope maker. In 1847, the homestead caught fire, and the present house was built for Newton Holcomb. Despite the additions of siding and bay windows, the general plan and proportions of the house remain. (DP.)

HAGUE HOUSE, 1917. According to the assessors, this home at 441 North Loomis Street, at the northwest corner with Honeypot Road, was constructed in 1887. At the time of this photograph, the owners were Percy and Margaret Elton. The identity of the child is unknown. Percy became the superintendent of the Springfield Water Department's West Parish facilities in Westfield and was very active in the Westfield River Watershed Association. For over 50 years, the home was owned by Jim and May Hague.

WALT SAUNDERS HOUSE, C. 1920. A colonial tavern was formerly at 201 College Highway, now the parking lot of Ocean State Job Lot. Between 1850–1880, it was replaced by this house, with its prominent overhang on the gable end and ornamental Victorian brackets. Gerald and Carolyn Cleary purchased the property in 1962, and shortly after, razed this and a nearby home. They built a driving range, par three golf course, and miniature golf course on the site. The property was later developed into an Ames department store and Big Y grocery store.

ELWIN "SHADY" HILLS HOUSE, C. 1995. The house at 26 College Highway, a short distance north of the state line, is the finest Colonial Revival home in Southwick. Built in 1906 at a cost of $5,000, roughly double what most homes cost at the time, it had steam heat, possibly a first for any residence in town. Hills was nicknamed "Shady" because of his knowledge of growing shade tobacco. Active in the Congregational church, he was a deacon there. Since his death in 1936, it has been owned by the Stromgren, Vangelder, Flagg, Thompson, and Feldman families.

Four

FARMS

SUNNYSIDE RANCH, C. 1980. Sunnyside Ranch at 65 Sunnyside Road was a prominent dairy farm. It was built in 1897–1899 as a model farm for Robert B. and James S. Crane. In the mid-1800s, the property was a source of wood for the local railroad when wood-fired engines and bridges demanded it. From 1922 to 1997, generations of the Hall family produced milk from a large herd of Holsteins. Since then, over 200 acres have been converted into a PGA golf course, the Ranch, which opened in July 2001. The timber-frame barns seen here were converted into a restaurant, pro shop, and pavilion for special events.

LITTLE GIRL WITH PIGS, C. 1925. Every farm had a few pigs. They were easy to raise as long as they were well-penned, and could be fed most table scraps, whey from cheese-making, or cooked root crops. Pigs were typically started in spring and put up in late fall or early winter. This picture was taken in late spring, based on the foliage and size of the piglets. The girl was tentatively identified as "Topsy" by the late Marilyn Gillett, the donor of the photograph.

DETAIL OF GEORGE STEERE BARN, 1985. Few barns from the 1700s survived in town to be photographed. At 18 Vining Hill Road, this example dated from the 1790s. Its robust beams and large braces supported this early date. After it was taken down, a new riding stable was constructed in the vicinity.

RAY FOWLER WALKING TO BARN, C. 1910. Taken behind the homestead at 739 College Highway, this photograph shows an English-style barn that was probably built about the time of the house, 1790. Large double doors opposite each other could be opened to create a breeze for hand winnowing chaff from grain. Hay would be stored to one side of the center aisle, while animals would be housed on the other side. The shed to the right may have housed carriages and tools. (DG.)

RAY FOWLER INSTRUCTING NEPHEW TO DRIVE HORSES, C. 1910. Imagine the joy and fear of Ray Fowler's nephew Grant Wilson as he guides this team of horses toward the barn, possibly the same one seen above. Thousands of boys learned the same way across the countryside. (DG.)

BARN, 20 DEPOT STREET, 1995. Another English-style barn, this one's center floor area had a huge windlass mounted in the upper framework in 1865 or shortly thereafter by members of the Phelps family, who were cattle merchants. Cattle were butchered there, and the windlass allowed the carcasses to be easily lifted to accelerate the process. The barn has since been razed. (LDH.)

ANDERSON FARM, AUTUMN 1946. This scene near the corner of Nicholson Hill Road and College Highway represents traditional farming. Shocks of cornstalks are in front of a hayfield, to the left is a tobacco barn, in the background is a pasture, and to the right is the main barn for hay, horses, and cattle. The shorter section to the right was a carriage shed and workshop. The tobacco barn collapsed in the 1960s, and the "Halloween Snowstorm" of October 29–30, 2011, which dumped 14.5 inches of heavy snow, collapsed most of the other buildings. None of them stand now.

BERTHA AND STEWART MILLER ON A DOODLEBUG, C. 1939. The doodlebug, or homemade tractor, was common around 1920–1945. Kits for converting cars into tractors were available, but a savvy farm mechanic with plenty of parts could strip a car down and convert it for nothing. Lack of cash during the Great Depression and scarcity of metal during World War II resulted in their popularity. The Millers used this doodlebug on their farm at 264 College Highway. (SMJ.)

BARN, 85 MORT VINING ROAD, C. 1921. The right section of this barn is roughly 200 years old and was constructed with a different level for the animals. The added ceiling height allowed for housing dairy cows or horses. Another feature inside the far right section, gone for years, was a round silo for storing chopped corn silage, probably dating from 1890 to 1910, making it one of the earliest-known Southwick silos. The left section was at one time used as a shop and carriage shed. (LDH.)

A Pair of Workhorses, c. 1920. While teams of oxen were the typical draft animals of New England farms until the mid-1800s, horses became the norm after the Civil War. They were able to do the same work faster, although their cost was greater. In this photograph, Arthur Gillett poses with his team, including one named Tim.

Cows Feeding, c. 1985. One of many dairy farms in town was Crestview Farm at 242 College Highway, owned by Walter Dziengelewski. A former tobacco barn was converted into a stanchion-style dairy barn. Around 1975, major changes were made, including a milking parlor, a concrete bunker silo replacing the upright silo, a liquid manure system, and this feed trough installed south of the barns. The herd was built up to about 100 head. Changes in the dairy industry resulted in its closing, and all animals and equipment were auctioned off in 1997. The buildings have been since razed.

PUTNAM FAMILY AND FARM SIGN, JULY 1957. Ten months after buying the farm at 249 College Highway, repairing barns, building up a flock of laying hens, and then designing and purchasing a sign, the Putnam Farm was about to open. From left to right are Jim II, Jim Sr., Charlie, John, Fran, and Steve Putnam. For years, the sign invited the public to their farm. Eggs were eventually replaced by vegetables, chicken pot pies, and baked goods. The family, several international students, and many locals worked there over its 40-plus years. It is presently owned by Lenita Boper and run as Blossoming Acres. (JP.)

PUTNAM BARN DURING RENOVATION. Stripped of its sheathing, the old bones of the barn frame are exposed. Toward the tops of the posts are diagonal braces to stiffen the framework, all held together with pegs. Built on a bank, the cellar may have been used for manure. The main doorway was apparently on the right side. Renovated by Paul Cigal for the Putnam family farm, it was repurposed as a bakery, tea room, and retail store, and is now Blossoming Acres. (JP.)

An Assortment of Barns, 1970s. During the 1800s and early 1900s, specialized barns were very common on farms. This collection of barns at 217 Sheep Pasture Road featured a bull barn to the left, a corn crib, carriage shed, workshop, and others. Changing agriculture practices and the costs of maintaining these buildings have diminished their presence.

Leon Barnes's Dairy Barn, c. 1930. The property at 707 College Highway was a showplace. Built in the early 1900s, it was a ground-level stable barn. The gambrel roof maximized hay space, concrete floors made it cleaner, and windows illuminated where the cows were stanchioned. Cupolas offered ventilation, and corn in the silo supplemented hay. The farm was owned by the Barnes family from 1864 to 1944 and Hatheway & Steane Corporation from 1944 to 1973. George Hughes was a farm manager there. It was converted into Chuck's Steak House, which operated for years, and is now Westfield River Brewing Co.

RAKING HAY, C. 1930. One of the most unusual Southwick photographs is this unidentified woman raking hay behind a single horse. The rake itself is possibly a "flop-rake" from the mid-1800s. The woman appears to be wearing either loose slacks or a long dress.

GETTING IN THE HAY, 1953. While baled hay was becoming common in the 1950s, small farms still depended on the pitchfork as harvesting equipment. With Marge Miller on the load and sister Sandra on the ground, this photograph proves that young women could be instrumental in bringing in fodder for the farm animals. The corner of the house visible at upper right was 87–89 Mort Vining Road. (SMJ.)

SOLEK FARM, LATE 1960S. This aerial view shows the barn, home, and some of the fields at 230 Granville Road. The Solek family came to Southwick in 1920. They initially had only a couple of cows and raised field tobacco. Walter Solek transitioned to dairy in earnest in 1965, eventually building up his herd to 100 head. Over the years, milk was sold to Casey's Dairy in Westfield, the New England Milk Producer's Association, Pioneer Dairy, and finally Agri-Mark in West Springfield. Solek lost at least five cows to coyote and bear.

SODOM MT. FARM. In 1982, Joseph and Judy Radwilowicz purchased the Lorenzo Lambson farm at 261 South Loomis Street. They built the dairy farm from scratch, putting up the main barn and Harvestore silos, and converting several tobacco barns for dry cows and hay storage. With 300 head of registered Holsteins, this was the largest dairy farm that ever existed in Southwick. For at least 10 years, the farm won the Massachusetts Dairy of Distinction Award.

Five

TOBACCO

COLLEGE HIGHWAY, 1921. Looking south toward the Methodist church and its former parsonage, a tobacco barn that would ultimately become the Dziengelewski dairy farm can be seen at 242 College Highway. While most tobacco barns were built on level ground, topography sometimes dictated that the barn be built to conform to the land. The dip in the road is where Pearl Brook flows. (KS.)

JOHN HORKUN SPEARING TOBACCO, LATE 1940S. A young John Horkun is seen here harvesting broadleaf or field tobacco. A number of rows have been cut and wilted, and he is spearing the stalks onto a lath, the most difficult job in the process. Virtually every farmer in the area tried to raise a few acres of field tobacco as a source of cash. By this time, the locally grown broadleaf tobacco was used as filler and binder for cigars, while the perfect outer wrapper was made from tobacco "grown under shade."

SOUTHWICK, 1919. The caption on this photograph does not say who is pictured here or where it is, but it is a typical scene in town; a small, flat field has been set with tobacco, and the harvest is nearing completion. The horse-drawn wagon appears to have been either converted for this particular use or repaired with several hastily nailed braces. The weight of the harvest and wagon requires a team of horses.

HARVEST COMPLETED, C. 1950. With the harvest done, the workers take a break and pose for the camera. While the man in the background is unidentified, the man standing at left is Donald Hamberg, and the boy is a neighbor, Gene Griffin. A flatbed truck was fitted for hauling tobacco instead of a two-wheeled trailer behind a tractor. The field is on the north side of Nicholson Hill Road. (LDH.)

A FILLED TOBACCO SHED. Across from the Westfield River Brewing Company is this tobacco barn filled with broadleaf tobacco. While the photograph was taken only a few years ago, it could have been taken 100 or more years ago in Southwick. (DG.)

STRIPPING TOBACCO, c. 1951. From left to right, Elsie, Harold, and Donald Hamberg are seen stripping the leaves from the stalks. The tobacco has already been drying for some time in the barn. Farmers waited until a rainy spell, or "tobacco damp," to strip the leaves in order to avoid breaking them. (LDH.)

DONALD HAMBERG, PRESSING TOBACCO, c. 1951. Once the leaves had been stripped from the stalk, they would be placed in a press, which would compact them into a rectangular bale. The bale would be tied, shipped, and sold. Further processing for cigars would be done elsewhere but typically included curing for flavor, additional sorting, and grading. (LDH.)

HATHEWAY & STEANE CORP. "C" FARM, BOX LOT, C. 1968. North of Feeding Hills Road, accessible by the driveway immediately west of the former railroad tracks, was the "C" Farm, which grew shade tobacco. Tobacco barns are in the background, along with a two-story mess hall and a separate kitchen. To the left are the seedbeds and piles of glazed sash. All of these buildings were demolished around 1971. (TA.)

FRED HANKS SEEDING THE BEDS, C. 1968. With the beds sterilized and the soil raked out, Fred Hanks is seeding the beds by hand. The beds will soon be covered with glazed sash to increase the warmth, the seeds will germinate, and the plants will be separated and then transplanted, or "set," in the field around Memorial Day. Years later, Hanks became a vice president for Roncari Construction and also served the community as a selectman, Democratic town committee chair, and American Legion commander, among other positions. (TA.)

TOBACCO BARN CONSTRUCTION, 1935. This series of photographs taken by Victor "Pete" Alvarez show just one of several styles of tobacco barn framing. Prior to these photographs being taken, several lines of poles were sunk into the ground and capped by a triple sill plate, outlining the long, outside walls of the shed. Next, scraps of blocks were nailed on top of the sill where they wanted each section of framing (referred to here as "bents") to end up. In the photograph above, the first bent has been raised and temporarily braced. Men with slender steel-pointed poles, or "pikes," helped push the bent up into place. Below, a series of bents have been raised and fixed in place. The ground posts and sills and the prefabricated bents are ready to go up. (Both, TA.)

BARN CONSTRUCTION CONTINUES. The next photograph shows the barn frame nearing completion. Note that the bents extend beyond the end of the sill and are supported on temporary blocks and framing in order to keep all the bents at the same height. In the final shot below, at least 26 proud men pose in front of their tobacco barn. Some of them had been the ground crew helping with pikes to raise the bents. Other workers were aerial carpenters nailing the sections together. A couple of men probably spiked the bents to the sills, while one or more coordinated the work. It took a big crew to frame a big barn. This one was constructed off South Longyard Road, in either Southwick or West Suffield, Connecticut. (Both, TA.)

AERIAL SPRAYING SHADE TOBACCO, C. 1970. This photograph shows a single-engine plane administering an application to a field of shade tobacco. (TA.)

FLORENCE "FLO" TYSZ, C. 1970. Walking through a tobacco barn with an armful of tissue paper, Flo Tysz is caught off guard by Terry Alvarez's camera. Tysz worked for the Hatheway & Steane Corporation, where her husband, Basil, was the manager of Farm "C" in Southwick. (TA.)

Six

CITIZENS

FIRST LT. RANSFORD W. KELLOGG. Son of Theodore M. and Helen (Bullock) Kellogg, Ransford attended Consolidated and Westfield High Schools and two years at Massachusetts State College. He enlisted in the US Army Air Corps, was commissioned a second lieutenant on May 22, 1944, and awarded his pilot wings. He was engaged to Evelyn Cass of Southwick in December 1944 and deployed the following January to pilot a B-24 bomber in the 8th Air Force in England, and promoted to first lieutenant in April. He completed 22 missions over Germany and northern Europe prior to Victory in Europe Day. On June 16, 1945, he and his crew were returning to the United States, but his B-24 was reported missing over the North Atlantic on June 17. The plane and its crew were never found. Kellogg was 22 years old. He was the last Southwick veteran killed in World War II, and in 1951, the new Southwick Veterans of Foreign Wars Post 872 adopted his name. (ME.)

REV. ABEL FORWARD. Born April 17, 1748, in Simsbury, Connecticut, Abel Forward was the sixth child of Deborah (Moore) and Lt. Abel Forward. He graduated from Yale in 1768, preached in Southwick in the summer of 1771, supplied preaching in present-day East Granby in 1773, and was ordained the first minister of the Southwick Congregational Church on October 27, 1773. He died on January 15, 1786. During his final illness, his second wife, Dorothy (Stiles) Forward, preached—a most unusual event. This headstone was carved by, or in the style of, William Crosby of Middletown, Connecticut. (PGB.)

RHODA LOOMIS. Another fine headstone is that of Rhoda Loomis. She was the wife of Revolutionary soldier Capt. Noah Loomis, who survived her, which may explain the term "consort." The upper section, or tympanum, is ornamented with a weeping willow and urn, both symbols of mourning in the very late 1700s and early 1800s. (PGB.)

MEDAL AWARDED TO AMASA HOLCOMB. Amasa Holcomb (1787–1875) was Southwick's renaissance man. Self-taught, he was an instructor at Suffield Academy by age 15, a surveyor, writer of several almanacs, Methodist lay preacher, and the first manufacturer of telescopes in the United States. In 1835, he traveled to the Franklin Institute in Philadelphia and showed his instruments to a team of respected scientists. He was awarded the Scott Premium for his telescope mount that made it easy to focus on an object with little vibration, also making it easier to track an object.

ROBERT CAMPBELL (1834–1926). A common sight on Gillett Road, now part of College Highway, was a dog pulling a wagon or sled with Robert Campbell in it. As an infant, Campbell contracted polio, lost all use of his lower legs, and would cross them and "walk" or climb stairs using his strong arms and hands for balance. He attended school, learned cigar-making, married, and raised three children. He enjoyed fishing from a boat and ice fishing from a sled, which he propelled with short spiked sticks, and kept a fine garden. He and his wife, Ellen (Cooley), celebrated their 66th anniversary a few months before he passed away.

25 Dollars REWARD!

STOLEN from the pasture of the subscriber, in Southwick, Ms. on the night of the 15th of Aug. inst., a light bay *MARE*, 7 years old, a white star in the forehead, off hind foot white to the fetterlock, switch tail, dark mane & tail: also an old fashioned saddle,----supposed to be taken by a man (name unknown) about 40 years of age, 5½ ft. high, rather dark complexion, spare face & dark eyes, had on a dark frock coat, black hat, and had a watch.

Whoever will take up said Thief and Mare, and return them to the subscriber, or give information where they may be taken, shall receive the above reward, or a reasonable compensation for either.

ABEL STEER.

Southwick, Ms. Aug. 20, 1842.

"25 DOLLARS REWARD!" ABEL STEERE (1791–1871). Stealing a horse was like stealing a car today. The reward would be the equivalent of $800. Abel Steere was born in Glocester, Rhode Island, on April 29, 1791, the son of Elisha and Lois (Aldrich) Steere. The family moved in 1795 by ox team and wagon and purchased land on the north side of Vining Hill Road. Abel married Alma Booth; the farm was divided, and he owned the western portion. He may have built the house at 72 Vining Hill Road. It is not known whether or not he recovered the horse.

EMILY (STEVENS) BOYLE (1811–1877). Emily was the second wife of John Boyle. Her younger sister Betsey Stevens (1807–1832) was his first wife. Emily was a devout Episcopalian, and the cross hanging from a chain alludes to her faith. She raised her sister's two children, as well as five of her own. One died in 1839, while three died of scarlet fever in 1850. Her surviving daughter, Jane, ultimately married William Phelps, and they lived at 20 Depot Street.

JOHN BOYLE (1803–1890). Born in Kilkenny, Ireland, John Boyle immigrated with his mother in 1819 to Canada, where she died. In 1826, he moved to Southwick, became a contractor for the construction of the New Haven to Northampton Canal, and later was a railroad and municipal contractor. Highly respected, he was elected to the Massachusetts House of Representatives in 1864. This portrait, along with that of Emily Boyle, most likely dates from the 1860s.

TARSUS NOBLE FOWLER (1805–1892). Tarsus was the grandson of Southwick's earliest known settler, Samuel Fowler. He later owned the Noble Fowler House, formerly at 739 College Highway. He was a farmer and served as a selectman in 1845. His sketch of the Fowlers in early Southwick provides some one-of-a-kind insights. Tarsus had this photograph taken in Westfield at Coleman Photography around 1885–1890. (DG.)

DR. FRED KNIGHT PORTER (1872–1916). Dr. Porter was one of only a handful of physicians who served Southwick for its first 150 years. Early-1900s records show he served as a doctor and a justice of the peace and was on the board of health. At a time when the selectmen oversaw public welfare, they paid for his services as a physician for the town poor. Porter was also said to be the town clerk, in charge of keeping birth and death records. He died at the age of 43.

WARD VINING (1826–1900). Serving during the Civil War in Company F of the 27th Massachusetts Volunteers, this is one of very few portraits of a Southwick Civil War veteran. He owned a farm at 233 Mort Vining Road, just a short distance east of his childhood home. His mother and father, Mary (Steere) and Samuel Vining, were instrumental in the founding of the Methodist church in town. Ward Vining and his wife had nine or more children. Mort Vining Road was named after one of his sons, Morton. His daughter Sarah Jane married Edward Gillett, the horticulturist.

EDWARD GILLETT (1849–1931). Edward Gillett grew up at Gillett's Corner and was always interested in nature, partly due to the influence of his mother. He spent three years at the Massachusetts Agricultural College in Amherst, studying horticulture, leaving in 1873. This depiction of him is probably from that period. He eventually started Gillett's Fern and Wild Flower Farm, which combined his love of nature and entrepreneurial spirit. His annual catalogs brought him business from across the country and around the world. He retired in 1926.

HAROLD J. ANDERSON (1891–1967). Born May 23, 1891, in Perham, Maine, Harold J. Anderson was the son of John and Hannah Anderson. The family moved to Southwick in 1904. During World War I, he served in the Army in the 2nd Construction Bricklaying Company, Air Service. He married Rose Sathory, and they had three children. He was a carpenter and dairy farmer, as well as a member of the Congregational church, American Legion Post 338, and Southwick Fire Department. Harold Anderson died in 1967.

ELI AND CLARENCE BIRGE HEADSTONE. This is the only zinc monument in the Old Cemetery. From about 1875 to 1914, the Monumental Bronze Company was the sole maker of these markers. One could choose the base, type of monument, inset panels (pictorial, floral or geometric), and custom lettered inserts. Their "stones" were promoted by various ads and licensed agents. After 1879, monuments were sandblasted to make them appear more stone-like. As long as they were not too heavy, they frequently look as good today as the day they were erected. (DP.)

LUCY H. GILLETT (1880–1975). One prominent individual from Southwick was Lucy Gillett. The daughter of Charles J. and Julia (Luck) Gillett, she was one of the nation's preeminent nutritionists. She chaired the White House Conference on Child Health and Protection in 1932. Her 1932 book *Nutrition Service in the Field* was the result of that conference. She wrote numerous other books, articles, and pamphlets dealing with nutrition, primarily targeting children and the poor, as well as countless reviews on diet-related books for professional journals.

FOOD FOR HEALTH'S SAKE. One of Lucy Gillett's prominent works was *Food for Health's Sake*, published by Funk & Wagnalls. It went through several editions and was translated into Chinese in 1939.

FOOD FOR HEALTH'S SAKE

What to Eat

BY
LUCY H. GILLETT, B.S., M.A.

Director, Nutrition Bureau, Association for Improving the
Conditions of the Poor, New York

NATIONAL HEALTH SERIES

EDITED BY THE
NATIONAL HEALTH COUNCIL

New York ● F&W ● *London*

FUNK & WAGNALLS COMPANY

CHARLES J. "C.J." GILLETT (1836–1923). Taken in the late 1910s, this photograph shows C.J. Gillett wearing typical farm clothes of the period. While he was known as the largest maker of cigars in Southwick, he also had chickens, some pigs, and perhaps a couple of cows to care for. He sold Gillett cigars from coast to coast, sometimes in the tens of thousands. He was responsible for the construction of the C.J. Gillett cigar factory, built in 1872, which is one of two buildings at the Southwick History Museum. He was the father of nutritionist Lucy H. Gillett.

TELEPHONE OPERATORS, C. 1954. Before dial telephone service arrived in June 1954, a telephone operator made the connection between callers. From left to right are (seated) Carolyn Lent, K. Miller, and Ellen Johnson; (standing) Rose S. Anderson, Jane (Sathory) Tuttle, and Sylvia Hamberg, chief operator. The switchboard was in the living room of 435 College Highway. (LDH.)

HELEN PHELPS (1907–2002). Helen Phelps was well known in town. She was a librarian, charter member of the historical society, and a postal worker, among other roles. This view shows her behind a sorting case when the post office was in the Bernardara House at 487 College Highway, and dates from before March 25, 1953. On that day, the post office was relocated to the corner of Bonnie View and College Highway, where Subway is now. The post office has moved two more times, and the Bernardara House was dismantled in 1978–1979 and eventually rebuilt in Connecticut.

SECOND LT. ROBERT LEE SYLVERNALE (1921–1945). The son of Robert F. and Lillian M. (Goddard) Silvernail, Robert enlisted in the US Army Air Force on January 28, 1943, was commissioned in February 1944, and earned his wings. After more training, he was assigned to the 490 Bomb Squadron, 341 Bomb Group, as a navigator. The squadron was known as the "Burma Bridgebusters." His parents received a telegram stating that their son had been missing since January 17 after not returning from a mission over the Burma-India area. His remains were never recovered.

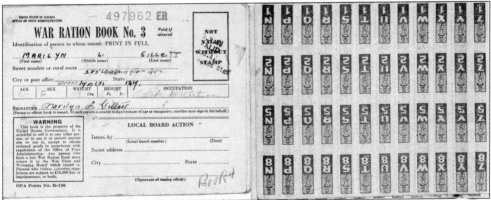

MARILYN GILLETT (1923–2008) WAR RATION BOOK. During World War II, the Office of Price Administration started rationing to ensure fair access to essential food and supplies. All Americans were issued ration books. When purchasing a rationed item, the merchant would remove a stamp from the book and take payment. If the item was worth less than the stamp, customers would receive a dime-sized fiber token. Newspapers published what particular stamps were worth because of changing needs during the war. Rationing made every civilian a part of the war effort.

CHARLES F. "CHAS" GILLETT (LEFT) AND FRIEND. Son of Arthur and Lillian (Johnson) Gillett, Chas Gillett (1921–1946) attended the Mooretown and Consolidated Schools and graduated from Westfield High School and Capitol Radio Engineering School in Washington, DC. He enlisted in September 1942 and became a ground crew mechanic in the bomber squadron of the 8th Army Air Corps out of England as a sergeant. After his honorable discharge, he fell sick, was hospitalized in the Veteran's Administration hospital in Bronx, New York, for two months, and died on April 5, 1946. His best friend, Douglas Hamberg, concluded that the health problems of Chas "were brought on or aggravated by the stress of serving overseas during war-time." His dog tags are pictured below.

FLORENCE JOHNSON (1920–2013), APRIL 1942. Daughter of Carl and Mabel Johnson, Florence attended local schools, graduated from Westfield High in 1937, and began work at the Springfield Armory in 1942. In April, she became the first woman to receive a Certificate for Outstanding Service in building M-1 rifles. She worked at the armory until 1945. In 1946, she married Walter Morgan, a former armory inspector and World War II veteran. They had two children. She was active in the Congregational church, historical society, and women's club, and both were active square dancers. (SA, NPS.)

TYOLA (KARLSTROM) PETRUSKA (1930–1988). Daughter of Maurice and Karin Marie Karlstrom, Tyola was born May 15, 1930, attended local schools, learned to play trumpet, and enlisted in the Women's Army Corps in 1949 under the promise that she could join a band. On March 5, the 14th Army Band (WAC) was restarted, and Tyola became a member. The band toured the country, including the Springfield Shriner's Hospital in 1951. She married another Army member, Michael Petruska Jr., in 1952 and ended her Army career in 1953. The mother of four, she died in 1988.

DEDICATION OF PRIFTI MEMORIAL PARK, 1981. Nuchi Prifti (1915–1980) was a lifelong town servant. Born in Springfield, his family moved to Southwick in 1917. He started Prifti Motors, was in the fire department, initiated the ambulance service, served on the school committee (including 22 years as chairman), was on four school building committees, and was a selectman. On September 27, 1981, the area north of Consolidated School was dedicated as the Nuchi T. Prifti Memorial Park. Pictured are John Viel and Vivian Brown, select board members. (D&NP)

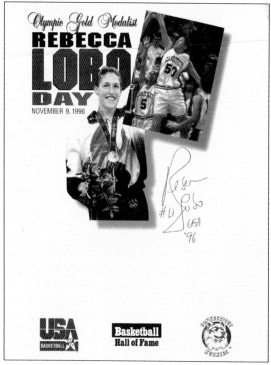

REBECCA LOBO-RUSHIN (BORN 1973). Daughter of Dennis and the late Ruth Ann Lobo, Rebecca was born in Hartford and lived in Granby, Connecticut, before the family moved to Southwick in 1975. She played basketball as a center at the Southwick Recreation Center; for Southwick-Tolland High School (1987–1991), earning a state record 2,740 points; the UConn Women Huskies (1991–1995), culminating in an NCAA championship; the 1996 gold-medal US Olympic women's basketball team; and in the Women's NBA (1997–2003). She was inducted into the Basketball Hall of fame in 2017. An author, ESPN commentator, wife, mother, and role model, she resides in Granby, Connecticut.

Seven

FOR THE PUBLIC BENEFIT

BEFORE COLLEGE HIGHWAY, 1921. By the 1910s, automobiles were here to stay, and better roads were imperative. Dirt roads were dusty in the summer, hip-deep in mud in the spring, and a frozen, rutted mess in winter. This view is from the yard of 2 Klaus Anderson, looking south on what was sometimes called "Gillett Road." The house on the left is the Lambson or Simcak House at 356 College Highway. Only a year or so after this photograph was taken, new bridges and drainage had been installed, and the road was regraded, paved, and renamed College Highway. (KS.)

METHODIST CHURCH EXTERIOR, 1918. Built after the 1823 fire that destroyed the first Congregational meetinghouse, the Methodist church was completed about 1825. The Episcopalians in town were predominantly responsible for raising the $2,000 to construct the edifice, but it was shared with the local Methodists. With the growth of Methodism and shrinking of the local Episcopal church membership, it shortly became a Methodist church. It once had a tall spire, which was destroyed by lighting in the 1890s, atop the tower base seen here, which was removed about 1950. (CCUM.)

METHODIST CHURCH INTERIOR, 1918. This interior looks like many churches built in the 1800s. The pulpit is on a raised platform, and the slip-pews are arranged in four rows with two aisles running from front to rear. The balconies had level floors and were set up for church suppers with folding chairs and tables. Five years after this photograph, the area between the balconies was infilled with joists and flooring to create a second floor, at which time the pews were relocated to the new second-floor sanctuary. The first floor was renovated for use as a social hall with a restroom and kitchen. (CCUM.)

OLD CEMETERY VAULT, 1872. The Old Cemetery was started in the early 1770s. Burials were impossible during the winter, so they may have used a nearby shed or corn house where coffins could be stored until spring. In 1854, the cemetery was enlarged to the rear, and in 1872, this brick and granite vault was finally built in the newer section. While picturesque, it has not been used for over 70 years. (DP.)

OUR LADY OF THE LAKE CHURCH, C. 1950. For 175 years, Southwick had no Catholic church. Mass was occasionally celebrated in various homes and other locations. On December 13, 1944, Daniel T. and Rose A. Keenan donated land on Sheep Pasture Road for a site. Construction was started on an interim basement chapel on September 1, 1947, and Mass was celebrated on Easter 1948. This postcard shows the church as it appeared from 1948 to 1961. A brick colonial-style sanctuary was erected atop the basement chapel in the latter year.

SPIRIT OF 76 JUNIORS, FIFE AND DRUM CORPS. Started around 1956–1957 by Aldo Cigal, the corps met in the rectory basement of Our Lady of the Lake Church. Many of the members were also in the church's Boy Scout troop, but at least a half-dozen girls were in the corps. The members played on metal fifes and drums made by Noble and Cooley of Granville. They marched in area parades and attended competitions at locations like Riverside Park in Agawam and Look Park in Northampton. By the fall of 1961, they no longer existed. (MP.)

CAMP FIRE GIRLS, C. 1915. Labeled "Council Meeting" in Maud Gillett's scrapbook, this photograph shows one of the earliest youth groups in Southwick, the Camp Fire Girls. Started in 1910 in Thetford, Vermont, it was nationally chartered in 1912. By December 1913, it boasted 60,00 members. The Southwick unit was organized about 1914. For several years, they were very active in town.

OWAISSA, C. 1915. This anglicized Ojibwe term, meaning "eastern blue bird," was popularized in Longfellow's poem "The Song of Hiawatha." The word had been adopted into Camp Fire Girls language and symbolism, and this member used it as her name or title. While the photograph was labeled "Maud Gillett," it is obvious that this is no 31-year-old woman. Her identity is a mystery. The wearing of a Native American–inspired dress for ceremonial purposes was normal for the Camp Fire Girls until a change in policy in 1946.

NORTH LONGYARD DISTRICT SCHOOL, C. 1925. With students gathered here and there, this is a very informal school photograph. Built in 1886, the North Longyard District School was one of five identical schools built that year. There were also four older ones and the Dickinson Grammar School. By 1916, there were 11 one-room schools and the Dickinson school. All were closed in May 1929 when Consolidated School opened. This schoolhouse and its land were sold in 1930, and the building was converted into a residence; it is now 36 North Longyard Road.

CONSOLIDATED SCHOOL BOYS BASKETBALL TEAM, 1940. Every championship team is a source of school pride. From left to right are (first row) Fred Piescharka, unidentified, Robert Arnold, Lyndel Maynard, and possibly Herbert Root; (second row) Fred Rutka, Donald Desmond, Raymond Tomasini, Dana Maynard (coach), Raymond Garcia, possibly Norman Chaffee, and possibly Fred Scholpp. (KS.)

SWEDISH CHURCH, NORTH GRANBY, 1921. In the late 1890s, Swedish families began buying farms in Southwick and North Granby. Wishing to have services in Swedish, in 1902, they formed the Free Christian Society of North Granby, purchased a 150-foot square plot for $1 on Loomis Street in Granby, and built a 25-foot-wide, 30-foot-deep church. A foyer with a steeple was added in 1903. In 1926, materials were salvaged from this edifice and used in building a new church at 605 Salmon Brook Street in Granby, which is now the Pilgrim Covenant Church. (LDH.)

HENDRICK S. AND SARA BRITA HAMBERG,
c. 1910. At least seven of the fourteen
original members of the Swedish church
were related by blood or marriage, with
a number living in Southwick. Hendrick
and Sara were charter members who had
moved from Sweden to Canada about
1880 and then bought a 53-acre farm at
126 South Loomis Street in Southwick
in 1900. On August 21, 1902, they were
elected the first deacons. (LDH.)

FLAGPOLE AND MARKER. During the
nation's bicentennial, a flag pole and
granite boulder with a bronze plaque
were installed inside the gates of the
Old Cemetery, courtesy of the Veteran
of Foreign Wars Post 872, American
Legion Post 338, and their auxiliaries.

BUS DRIVERS, 1940–1941. This is one of the few photographs of Southwick bus drivers. The bus routes were not only for Consolidated School, which had opened in May 1929, but also for students attending Westfield High School, since Southwick did not have one. The four drivers are, from left to right, Clarence Hudson, Lawrence Johnson, Ralph Deming, and Albert Drake Sr.

LIONS PEE WEE CHAMPIONS, 1953. Prior to the Southwick Recreation Center in 1961, local organizations and businesses independently sponsored youth baseball teams. "Pee Wee" was a generic term with no affiliation to the Little League, which traced its existence to 1939. This team's sponsors, the Southwick Lions Club, has been chartered since April 2, 1947. It still supports youth sports, scholarships, and eyesight-related issues. This is the winning team for 1953, in their uniforms with Lions Club patches, and their coach Jim Phelps. (MP.)

INSTALLATION OF FIRST VFW COMMANDER, 1951. Prior to May 29, 1951, some Southwick veterans had belonged to the Granville Veterans of Foreign Wars post. On that date, the Ransford W. Kellogg Post No. 872 of the VFW was organized at the Southwick Country Club. From left to right are town moderator Lorenzo Lambson, selectmen Towar Arnold and Danny Salvatico, newly installed VFW post commander Ralph Liptak, and state representative Anthony Parenzo. (JM.)

DEDICATION OF VETERAN MARKER, BETWEEN 1952 AND 1956. Prior to the addition of the wings to the granite veteran memorial, the VFW and auxiliary installed a small granite marker with a bronze plaque on the town common. While unlabeled, these representatives are believed to be, from left to right, Geraldine Krawczyk, Ralph Liptak, Raymond Elton, and Irving Martin.

VFW Honor Guard, Early 1950s. Both the VFW and American Legion have always had honor guards for parades and ceremonies. It is believed that this photograph dates from the early 1950s.

Southwick Police Association, 1955. In early 1955, the police association was formed to support the police department and community. Its first annual ball was held at the new junior high school auditorium on April 15 of that year. From left to right are (first row, seated) Charles Jones, treasurer; Michael D. Sullivan, secretary; Chief Harold Hamberg, selectman; Constable Joseph Moorehouse, president; and Constable Adam J. Konopka, vice president; (second row, standing) officers George Millot, H.C. Hansen, Harry Burdick, Gerald Celley, and Frank Zomek.

LADIES AUXILIARY CHARTER, 1951. Dated December 1, 1951, this charter legally established the auxiliary with its original 22 members. (JM.)

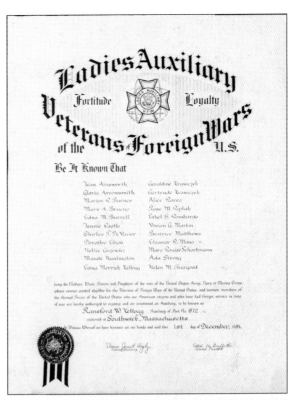

VFW POST 872 AUXILIARY, c. 1952. Members of the newly formed auxiliary pose on the stage of Consolidated School. From left to right are (seated) Geraldine Krawczyk, Rose Liptak, Gertrude Krawczyk, Louise Massoia, Mary Skemans, Florence Flesher, Ada Strong, and Mary Brueno; (standing) Mrs. Kellogg, Vivian Martin, Gloria Arrowsmith, Marion Barnes, Eleanor Mono, Helen Thurgood, Edna Burrill, Maude Huntington, and Jennie Castle. (JM.)

Boy Scout Troop 118, Memorial Day, c. 1952. The second Boy Scout unit organized in town was Troop 118, sponsored by the Methodist church, in the fall of 1942. From left to right are Gordon Wolfe, Frederick Kellogg, Clifford "Kip" Sponberg Jr., Robert Van Mater, and unidentified.

Boy Scout Eagle Court of Honor, 1994. Over the years, numerous Southwick Scouts have achieved the highest rank of Eagle, at several times the national average. This photograph shows two younger Scouts, R.J. Ligenza (left) and Chris Pike, assisting in an Eagle Court of Honor ceremony for three older Troop 114 Scouts who were about to be presented their Eagle badges. (SR.)

VIVIAN AND BOB SATTLER, C. 1975. On October 26, 1951, nine railroad enthusiasts met in the West Springfield home of B.W. Barnfather, formed the Western New England Live Steamers, and discussed acquiring land in Southwick on which to build a track for their miniature trains. On February 5, 1952, they formally organized and called themselves the Pioneer Valley Live Steamers. They leased land from Leslie Fowler at 108 Hillside Road but by late 1964 owned the property, which today totals over 10 acres. In this photograph are two early members of the group, Vivian and Bob Sattler. (PVLS.)

PVLS TURNTABLE. In addition to several different gauge tracks and a clubhouse is this turntable, which allows an engine to be turned around. While the engine here is steam-powered, other models use other fuels. All of the engines and cars are custom made by railroad enthusiasts, functional, and allow one or more people to ride the train. The club has always been open to the public on Father's Day weekend and another weekend in September. (PVLS.)

JUNIOR-SENIOR HIGH SCHOOL, 1960–1961. Southwick experienced extraordinary growth after World War II, along with an increase in students. An addition was made to Consolidated School in 1949–1950, a junior high school was built in 1953–1954, Woodland Elementary School was constructed by September 1958, and a high school addition went up in 1959–1960. This aerial view shows the junior-senior high school from the northwest. The lighter-colored roofs were the new high school addition. It was dedicated on April 16, 1961. This is now Powder Mill Middle School.

NEW HIGH SCHOOL, 1971. Continued growth demanded a new high school, so a building committee was formed on March 20, 1967. It recommended that the former junior-senior high school be used as a middle school, with a separate building for the high school students. The plan was rejected at a special town meeting because of cost, but was eventually accepted after scaling back. A proposed swimming pool building, outlined on the far right, was never built.

EXECUTIVE BOARD, SOUTHWICK HISTORICAL SOCIETY, C. 1972. When the town celebrated its 200th anniversary in 1970, it published a bicentennial history and had an exhibit of historical items. This fueled a desire for a historical society, which formed in 1971. This photograph is of an early executive board. From left to right are (first row, seated) Merrill Mason, Helen James, Merwin Tuttle, and Helen Phelps; (second row, standing) Paul Baillieul, Helen Arnold, Laura Fuller, David Anderson, and Clifford Sponberg.

SOUTHWICK GRANGE NO. 46. The grange was chartered in 1874, became inactive, and reorganized in 1921. It allows men, women, and youth of 14 as members and promotes rural education and improvements. It met in the Dickinson and Consolidated Schools. In 1957, Ren Sefton donated a lot behind Best Auto where the grange built this meeting hall. The members intended to build a first floor, which never materialized. This view shows the hall prior to an addition and gable roof. It is still an active organization.

MOTOCROSS 338 ("WICK 338"). In 1972, Bernie Yelin gathered some fathers from American Legion Post 338, including Clovis Goyette, Pat Smith, Dante Molta, Ray Peebles, and others, and with shovels, chainsaws, and pickaxes created one of the best motocross tracks in the country. The first race was held April 1, 1973. In 1976, the course was added to the American Motorcyclist Association Motocross Nationals. This photograph, with a letter on the back from the Southwick Board of Selectmen, was a promotional item from the late 1970s.

MOTOCROSS 338, FIRST CURVE, 1981. Once the backward falling start gate has dropped, getting the lead around the first curve can be an emotional and physical plus for a rider. Early views of Southwick racing are difficult to find. Through parking fees, collection of returnable bottles and cans, distributing programs, and other opportunities, the motocross has given or generated tens of thousands of dollars for local charities, while the thousands of spectators and racing teams have patronized local businesses. (SR.)

THE GORGE. One of the most picturesque spots in Southwick is the Gorge. Cut by Munn Brook, it represents the break between Sodom Mountain to the south and Drake Mountain to the north. Several local swimming holes are to the west of this view. The Town of Southwick acquired this parcel in 1980, with the Conservation Commission overseeing it. In this general vicinity was a sawmill in the mid-1800s. (LDH.)

GROUND-BREAKING CEREMONY, RAIL TRAIL. This is the May 12, 2008, ceremony for conversion of the abandoned railroad line into a bikeway. In front is Selectman Art Pinell. Behind him in the second row, from left to right are a Massachusetts Department of Transportation representative; a Lane Construction Company representative; state representative Rosemary Sandlin; Selectman Roger Cataldo; Jeff McCollough of the Pioneer Valley Planning Commission; Sue Pac, a Southwick gifted and talented teacher; US representative John Olver's liaison; and Lori Whitlock of the Park and Recreation Commission. (SHC.)

SGT. KEVIN BISHOP AND PATROLMAN RICHARD CROSS, 1994. Until World War II, law enforcement in Southwick consisted of constables appointed by the select board or town meeting. With tremendous population growth, Southwick developed a police department to address changing needs. Here, Sergeant Bishop converses with patrolman Richard Cross, who retired on September 29, 2012. Bishop was appointed chief of police in 2018. (SR.)

Eight

THE CONGAMOND LAKES

THE LAKE HOUSE, C. 1905. By the late 1800s, this was one of two hotels on the Congamond Lakes. At 127 Congamond Road, it provided great views of the Middle Pond, especially from the third-floor veranda. The various wings and types of windows suggest a structure that grew over the years. It was destroyed by fire in early 1927, and the Franklin House was built on the same site by Charles and Marion Franklin. (LDH.)

CANAL AT ISLAND. When the New Haven to Northampton, or Hampshire and Hampden Canal was constructed through Southwick, it entered South Pond going along the western shore, cut through the swampy peninsula of the southeast portion of Middle Pond, then across an 800-foot-long pontoon bridge of diagonally laid timbers to the western point on Middle Pond. A canal was dug across that peninsula to cut down on distance, thus creating the island at the end of Island Pond Road. This is a view of the canal today, although it has changed little since the late 1820s. (LDH.)

SOUTHWICK, JULY 29, 1885. While many people have appreciated the Congamond Lakes, the railroad made access easy and affordable. Beginning in the 1870s, the railroad company actively marketed the beauty of the lakes, targeting families, Sunday schools, and organizations. This tintype was undoubtedly taken by a photographer who was set up at one of the venues around the lake. (LDH.)

POINT GROVE ROAD, OR CHAPMAN'S BRIDGE, C. 1905. This photograph is just one of about a half dozen different postcards of Chapman's Bridge, named after John Chapman, who owned the dock on the other side of the bridge.

STEAMBOAT *HOLYOKE*, C. 1905. One of several steamboats owned by John Chapman, the *Holyoke* plied the waters of the Middle Pond of the Congamond Lakes during the late 19th and early 20th centuries. His daughter Edith was a pilot for this and his other boats. At the northernmost end of the pond, in the background is Chapman's Bridge, where Middle and North Ponds meet, and the wooden guardrail for Point Grove Road. (LDH.)

ELEVATOR TO WALKER ICE HOUSE, EARLY 1900S. Commercial ice harvesting started on the Congamond Lakes after the Civil War. By the early 1900s, there were five huge icehouses, which held a combined 225,000 tons of ice. The Walker Ice House was just north of the island on Middle Pond. This double elevator could be adjusted to bring the ice to any level in the icehouse.

WALKER RUN, EARLY 1900S. The photographer has walked almost to the top of the side ramp on the elevator in order to record this view. Despite shooting into the sun, blocks of ice and the tines on the elevator chain can be seen, which engaged the blocks of ice.

REAR VIEW OF ICEHOUSE, EARLY 1900S. The typical commercial icehouse in Southwick held 50,000–60,000 tons of ice and covered two acres. This one is undoubtedly the Walker Ice House. Taken from the rear or land side, the photograph shows a small pile of waste ice, the tower, and power plant, which generated the steam to run the conveyor. The horse-drawn carriages allude to the early date ascribed to this view.

ICEHOUSE ELEVATOR IN SPRING/SUMMER, c. 1910. This photograph appears to be of a different elevator than the previous shots. The man standing at the bottom gives an idea of the scale of the elevator. A walkway or ramp can be seen going up the right side of the elevator as well as on the ground.

TOP OF THE TOBOGGAN, MILLER'S BEACH, 1920S. A favorite spot was Miller's Beach on the Suffield side of South Pond. One of the draws was the "toboggan," which consisted of a wooden sled, or toboggan, with wheels that went down a sloped wooden track with guides into the lake. Babbs Beach had a similar ride. This view shows a couple on one toboggan just taking off from the top. (LDH.)

BOTTOM OF THE TOBOGGAN, MILLER'S BEACH. In this image, the photographer is shooting from a boat as a couple hits the water. This view gives a better idea of the height and length of the track. To the left is a dock stacked with more toboggans. The beach is said to have closed after a toboggan fatality. (LDH.)

CAMP MISHNOAH, c. 1922. Prior to the summer of 1921, the Springfield Women's Club purchased land on Congamond and constructed this camp for disadvantaged Springfield girls, which they operated until 1923. The Springfield Girls Club took over from 1924 to 1926. Because they were overseeing two camps and the logistics were too much, the Southwick camp was closed after the 1926 camp year. This postcard shows Camp Mishnoah in Southwick as a large bungalow with a screened-in basement and at least one canvas-wall tent to the left. (LDH.)

BOAT LANDING. The budding foliage alludes to spring, shortly before the crowds arrived at King's Sandy Beach. A number of rowboats were available, awaiting fishermen and tourists. Row boating was extraordinarily popular in the 19th and early 20th century and only waned with the increased availability of outboard motors, aluminum and fiberglass canoes, jet skis, and pontoon boats.

PITT GIGUERE, 1927. By the 1920s, numerous cottages and small homes, along with boat docks, had been built on North Pond. Pitt Giguere is shown here bailing water out of one of his rowboats. In the left background is the "Point" where North Pond broadens out to the east.

REFLECTION SCENE, SANDY BEACH. The peace and serenity of the "Sandy Beach," better known as King's Beach, is captured in this 1920s postcard view. After years of negotiation, the formation of the organization Conserve North Pond, and several town appropriations from the Community Preservation and General Funds, on June 28, 2019, Southwick formally took title to this parcel for open space.

White Hawk Cottage, 1930s. One of the early subdivisions in Southwick was Bungalow Heights in 1915. It consisted of Lakemont and most of Bungalow Streets. Individual lots were only 25 feet wide, so most folks wishing to build a cottage bought two or more parcels. This cottage on Lakemont Street, owned by Albert and Beatrice Marotta, was typical, with a simple gable roof, chimney for a stove or space heater, and screened-in porch. (CO.)

WATERCOLOR OF GINO'S BRASS RAIL. Louis "Gino" Boccasile purchased this land in 1939. According to the assessor's records, Gino's Brass Rail was built in 1945. Benjamin F. Babb had a horse-powered merry-go-round enclosed in an octagonal building on the same site on a small hill. An old photograph from *Bicentennial Book* shows not only the merry-go-round house, but also a sign that reads, "Brass Rail." Prior to Gino's, the ride and hill were removed. Boccasile retained the name of the previous business.

BRASS RAIL MENU. No restaurant in town at the time could compare with the Brass Rail. The main dining room could hold 250. It had a separate bar, a pavilion, a bowling alley, a nice location near the lake, and fine food. The pen and ink drawing on the menu highlighted just one of several stone fireplaces in the facility. The telephone number, 79-2, predates dial service that began on June 9, 1954.

FOOD MENU • SANDWICHES • SPECIAL TO ORDER

Brass Rail

Congamond Lakes   Phone 79-2   Southwick, Mass.

OAK KNOLL. By the early 1900s, lake cottages were being built on land not owned by the ice companies. This one was on property owned by Nelson Babb. An identical postcard, postmarked March 2, 1908, reads, "Your Summer Home, very best of wishes to you both from all of us at Cottage Grove. Nelson W. Babb." Cottage Grove was the early name for Babb's Beach. (LDH.)

PRIVATE ICEHOUSE, C. 1920. This is an example of a small private icehouse on North Pond. It could have been owned by one of the Kings or possibly Dan Keenan, who was known to have built one in that vicinity to provide ice to neighbors.

HERB DE GRAY, 1951. This photograph of the son-in-law of Sylvia and Arthur Giguere, who lived on Lakemont Street, was taken prior to Herb's deployment during the Korean Conflict (1950–1953). Bungalow Street is in the background. The dog, Smooky, is grinning from ear to ear. (CO.)

THE LILY POND AND CANAL TOWPATH, EARLY 1950S. About 1827, construction started on the Southwick portion of the New Haven to Northampton Canal. An earthen towpath was constructed 35 feet from the shore of Congamond. Most portions of the towpath had been removed over time, but sections survived in North Pond into the 1950s. The southern part of the pond was narrow, shallow, and known as "the Lily Pond," shown here. In the center is the towpath island, which had wild blueberries. Kids would swim to the island and munch on them. (JM.)

SOUTH POND BEACH AND PARK, 1992. In the early 1930s, it was Roxie's, but in late 1936, Harmon and Evelyn Smith bought Smith's Beach. In May 1941, Charlie Baiardi of West Springfield purchased the area and married Alice Hubert in 1942. During World War II, she ran the beach while he trained paratroopers. He returned after an injury and continued building and making improvements. In 1964, the Biardis retired and sold the property. After changing owners, recreation patterns, and arson, the property was sold to the Town of Southwick in 1986, which built the present structures. (SR.)

PONTOON BOAT REFURBISHMENT, 1996. Dick Grannells, past chair of the Lake Management Committee, is seen working on a pontoon boat. The committee has worked on lake safety issues and management of the two boat launches and has had a close relationship with the group Citizens Restoring Congamond. (SR.)

CRABBY JOE'S, 141 CONGAMOND ROAD. Few businesses in town have had more additions than this one. On April 6, 1937, Ovide H. Cote of Springfield, a World War I veteran, purchased the main parcel. He designed and built at least part of the restaurant known as Ovid's, which was known for fine food and a popular night club. It has operated under numerous names since then. A new restaurant plan submitted in 2019 calls for razing the existing building. (NBC.)

Nine

THE 1955 FLOOD

NORTH POND WASHOUT, AUGUST 20, 1955. After the New Haven to Northampton Canal was discontinued in 1847, a dike was built at the north end of North Pond. On August 17–19, 1955, Hurricane Diane dumped 19 inches of rain on Southwick. About 10:00 p.m. on August 19, the dike was breached, and the homes of Daniel Keenan and Bernard Drummond were washed away. This view shows a torrent of water, although the erosion suggests that the water had been at least three or four feet deeper. It is unknown whose boat dock is in the picture. (JM.)

SANDBAGGING, AUGUST 20, 1955. According to the late Nuchi Prifti, sandbagging on the culvert between Middle and North Ponds was started shortly after midnight and completed by mid-morning of August 20. This view must have been taken early that morning and shows countless men at work. Above the car to the left is the sign for Gino's Brass Rail. (JM.)

HIGH AND DRY. Water in Congamond was said to be six or more feet higher than normal, as evidenced by this North Pond boat left high and dry. Shortly after this, the dike was washed out, and much of North Pond was a virtual mud puddle for the next few years. (JM.)

114

BERNARD DRUMMOND HOUSE. The elevated lake level combined with the washed-out dike meant no hope for the Drummond house. The family had fortunately been evacuated, but their home, which was only a few years old, was totaled. This photograph was taken by Robert Keith Warriner of Southwick only a day or two after the washout.

WASHOUT AT SOUTH LONGYARD ROAD. The draining of North Pond created a chasm across South Longyard that could not be crossed for some time. The Drummond House had been to the right, but was washed downhill. On the other side is a man standing beside the Drummond mailbox. There were no more postal deliveries there.

SOUTH LONGYARD ROAD. The twisted steel culvert and cable suggest that this is approximately where South Longyard once was. The culvert ran under the road for stormwater but could not handle the flow from Hurricane Diane. A factor that made this storm worse was that only a few days earlier, Hurricane Connie had soaked the region. The rains of Hurricane Diane immediately became runoff.

SUSPENDED TRAIN SERVICE. One result of the flood was the washout of the sandy soils under this section of the New York, New Haven & Hartford Railroad. One or more boys are known to have crossed this washout on these tracks, although not with the permission or knowledge of mom or dad. This photograph, taken a little south of Depot Street, was developed in March 1956.

STRANDED. While there is still water in the main portion of North Pond, being almost 50 feet deep, the shoreline is so far removed from where it should be that every boat is stranded from the pond. King's Beach never recovered after the flood.

AT THE TOP OF THE WASHOUT. There is still debris floating on the pond and water flowing out of its Hurricane Diane–made channel. Former county engineer department records, now in the Registry of Deeds, suggest that the North Pond dike was rebuilt in May or early June 1957. At the same time, the dike at the end of South Pond was made more robust, and a double box culvert for the original Great Brook outlet was either completed or about to be installed. (JM.)

BULLDOZING THE TOWPATH AND LILY POND. In 1956, the remains of the old canal towpath/island just past North Lake Avenue were bulldozed away, and the pond resculpted. There would never again be blueberries picked there. (JM.)

LORENZO D. "L.D." LAMBSON ON A BULLDOZER. Every part of the region was affected by Hurricane Diane. Saunders Boat Livery on Middle Pond was destroyed, temporary bridges had to be installed, and farmland was devastated. Here, L.D. Lambson is about to do some cleanup with a small bulldozer. Topsoil was redeposited everywhere, and many crops were destroyed by the rains. (JP.)

FRED KELLOGG FARM, NORTH LOOMIS STREET. Every single brook overflowed its banks, including Munn Brook in the northwest part of town. Any grass or crop on this field was utterly stripped, along with tons of topsoil. Areas in the middle look like beach sand. It should be noted that the landscape looked even worse before this photograph, but the farmer had already begun regrading. (JP.)

Ten

I LOVE A PARADE

FIRST CAMP FIRE FLOAT. From about 1914, this postcard was in Maud Gillett's photograph album. Her father, amateur photographer Edward Gillett, was undoubtedly responsible for it. Maud was the adult leader, or guardian, with the Camp Fire Girls program in Southwick. In the background is the Hotel Southwick.

CONGAMUCK CAMP FIRE GIRLS. It is Memorial Day 1915 or 1916, and the Camp Fire Girls have put together a parade float, using the same wagon and edging as their first one. Congamuck is the earlier name for the Congamond Lakes used by the indigenous people and means "long fishing weir."

FLAGS OF THE NATIONS. The women on this stand or float represented the International Red Cross during World War I. France, the United States, and Belgium are in the first row, with Italy and England in the back. Prominently missing was Germany. By the end of the war, eight million Americans had volunteered for the American Red Cross.

YOUNG PATRIOTS. This World War I–era parade was either on Memorial Day or the Fourth of July. The automobile is filled with children, one in a "uniform" holding the American flag, and the young woman appears to represent Miss Liberty, although the device in her hand is less than torch-like. The building at far right is the Baptist church.

194 FORD F-6 CHASSIS COLEMAN ALL WHEEL DRIVE	HIGH PRESSURE FMC - JOHN BEAN	SOUTHWICK, MASS.

1948 FORD JOHN BEAN HIGH-PRESSURE FIRE ENGINE. In 1948, the select board ordered the fire equipment seen here. The front bumper sign reads, "Southwick Firemen's Association/Parade and Carnival/July 24, 25 26 Station Grounds," which dates this photograph to 1952. In the firehouse bay behind the apparatus, firemen socialize, while to the left is a carnival ride. (MR.)

SOUTHWICK FIREMEN'S PARADE, 1994. Leading the parade is engine No. 1 of the Southwick Fire Department, followed by ladder No. 1 and other equipment and units. For decades, the parade stepped off on Saturday evening and was the pinnacle of the annual Firemen's Carnival. (SR.)

RANSFORD W. KELLOGG POST NO. 872, VETERANS OF FOREIGN WARS. The VFW post is marching in the 1955 Fourth of July parade. All of these veterans served during World War II or Korea. They were marching south on College Highway past where Friendly's, now the Summer House, would later be built. Southwick Hill is behind them. (JM.)

WINNER OF BICYCLE PARADE, JULY 3, 1955. Barry Dill, son of Mr. and Mrs. Harry Dill, is pictured here. Children's events included the decorated bicycle competition, 25-, 50-, and 75- yard dashes, golf ball, and tire and sack races, complemented by hot dogs, soda, and ice cream. There was also a color guard competition and a free concert on the Consolidated School grounds by the Whip City Post Drum Corps. (JM.)

SPECIAL SOUTHWICK BICENTENNIAL FLOAT, 1970. A beauty pageant was held to crown a bicentennial queen for the town. Sixteen-year-old Elizabeth Meunier was selected and is pictured with her court, which included Mary Ellen Maloney, Lynn Ellershaw, Pauline Isabelle, and Jolene Baker.

PIONEER DAIRY FLOAT AND MILK TRUCK. Atop this 1970 parade float is the wooden-wheeled delivery wagon with the sign reading "From This," followed by the modern tanker truck with a sign reading "To This." At the time, Pioneer Dairy had been in business for 50 years. (RB.)

"OUR FIRST SAWMILL 1920's." The old carriage to the Battistoni sawmill was cleaned up, painted, and set on their delivery truck as part of the Southwick bicentennial parade. The buildings in the background were part of the Battistoni lumberyard at 61 Granville Road. (RB.)

FROM ATOP THE FERRIS WHEEL, 1976. The Southwick Firemen's Carnival combined commercial rides and concessions with those run by the firemen and their families. They included a dime toss, softball in the milk can, turtle races, and a dunking booth. This photograph was probably taken on a Friday evening; Saturday would have been far more crowded.

SOUTHWICK PUBLIC LIBRARY CENTENNIAL PARADE. On July 11, 1992, the library sponsored a parade to celebrate 100 years of service. Representatives from the fire department included Deputy Chief Rick Anderson (left), Spray the Dalmatian, and Jim D'Onofrio. Anderson later served as fire chief from 2010 to 2016. (SR.)

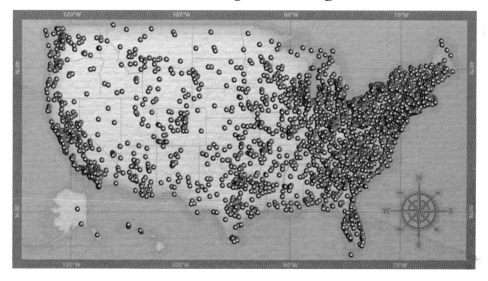